Glow-in-the-Dark Animals

PLANKTON

Ryan Nagelhout

PowerKiDS press.

New York

Published in 2015 by The Rosen Publishing Group, Inc.
29 East 21st Street, New York, NY 10010

First Edition

Editor: Katie Kawa
Book Design: Katelyn Heinle

Photo Credits: Cover Purestock/Thinkstock.com; cover, pp. 1–24 (background texture) olesya k/Shutterstock.com; pp. 4–5 Alexander S. Kunz/Moment/Getty Images; pp. 6–7 Brandon Rosenblum/Moment Open/Getty Images; p. 6 (phytoplankton) http://commons.wikimedia.org/wiki/File:Diatoms_through_the_microscope.jpg; p. 6 (zooplankton) http://en.wikipedia.org/wiki/Zooplankton#mediaviewer/File:Copepodkils.jpg; pp. 8–9 DuongMinhTien/Shutterstock.com; pp. 10–11 Stocktrek Images/Getty Images; pp. 12–13, 14–15 Visuals Unlimited, Inc./Wim van Egmond./Visuals Unlimited/Getty Images; pp. 16–17 Ethan Daniels/Shutterstock.com; pp. 18–19 © iStockphoto.com/bbsferrari; pp. 20–21 Per-Andre Hoffmann/Picture Press/Getty Images; p. 22 © iStockphoto.com/bjonesmedia.

Library of Congress Cataloging-in-Publication Data

Nagelhout, Ryan, author.
 Plankton / Ryan Nagelhout.
    pages cm. — (Glow-in-the-dark animals)
 Includes bibliographical references and index.
 ISBN 978-1-4994-0177-6 (pbk.)
 ISBN 978-1-4994-0179-0 (6 pack)
 ISBN 978-1-4994-0175-2 (library binding)
 1. Marine plankton—Juvenile literature. 2. Bioluminescence—Juvenile literature. I. Title.
 QH91.8.P5N34 2015
 578.77'6—dc23
                                    2014030408

Manufactured in the United States of America

CPSIA Compliance Information: Batch #CW15PK: For Further Information contact Rosen Publishing, New York, New York at 1-800-237-9932

CONTENTS

GLOWING WAVES

Have you ever stood on the beach at night and watched the water rush to your feet? What would you think if that water was glowing? Would you think something bad was put into the water? Would you worry the water wasn't safe for swimming?

In some parts of the world, water glows because of tiny creatures called plankton. There are more than a million species, or kinds, of plankton. Some special kinds have **chemicals** that cause them to glow at night. Why do they glow? Where can we find this glowing plankton? Read on to find out!

These waves are glowing because they're home to glowing plankton.

PLANT OR ANIMAL?

Plankton are tiny **organisms** that live in the ocean and sometimes in freshwater. "Plankton" is a general term for different organisms, such as **algae**, bacteria, and other tiny animals. Because they're too small or too weak to swim, they float and drift with the water's current.

Plantlike plankton are called phytoplankton. Animallike plankton are zooplankton. Glowing plankton live in oceans, usually in warmer waters. The glowing plankton we see from beaches live close to shore in **shallow** waters, but glowing plankton live throughout the oceans as well.

phytoplankton

zooplankton

Most plankton can't be seen unless they glow.

NEWS FLASH!

Scientists don't know why there aren't any freshwater glowing plankton. Some think freshwater plankton don't have certain chemicals that cause the glowing.

HOW SMALL ARE THEY?

Just how tiny are plankton? They're tiny enough that thousands of them fit inside a single drop of water! Many are so small they can't even be seen without a **microscope**. There are three basic sizes of plankton. The largest, called macroplankton, can be over 0.04 inch (1 mm) long and can be caught in nets.

Some plankton can be caught in fishing nets. Nannoplankton can't be caught in any kind of net.

Plankton from 0.002 to 0.04 inch (0.05 to 1 mm) long are called microplankton, a group that includes both phytoplankton and zooplankton. The smallest plankton, called nannoplankton or dwarf plankton, are less than 0.002 inch (0.05 mm) long. Most nannoplankton are plantlike.

NEWS FLASH!

Phytoplankton are too small to be considered macroplankton.

HOW DO THEY GLOW?

Plankton glow because of a **process** called bioluminescence (by-oh-loo-muh-NEH-suhns). The word comes from "bio," which means "life," and "lumen," which means "light." A bioluminescent animal is one that makes its own light! It does this with the help of special chemicals in its body.

Many different kinds of plankton make their own light. Plankton usually make blue or green light. Scientists think plankton only create light at night because they only use their ability to create light when it's needed. They don't need light often during the day.

During the day, some kinds of algae can turn the water red. At night, these same plankton make the water glow!

11

WHY SO BRIGHT?

Plankton glow to stay safe. Many animals that live in oceans eat plankton. Plankton can feel when the water around them moves. They think the motion is caused by a predator, so they create a flash of light with their body. Plankton use their light flashes to scare off animals that are trying to eat them.

Scientists also think plankton's flashes could actually be used to **attract** fish larger than the ones hunting them. These larger predators would eat the fish hunting the plankton.

Bioluminescence is a common way ocean creatures keep themselves safe from predators.

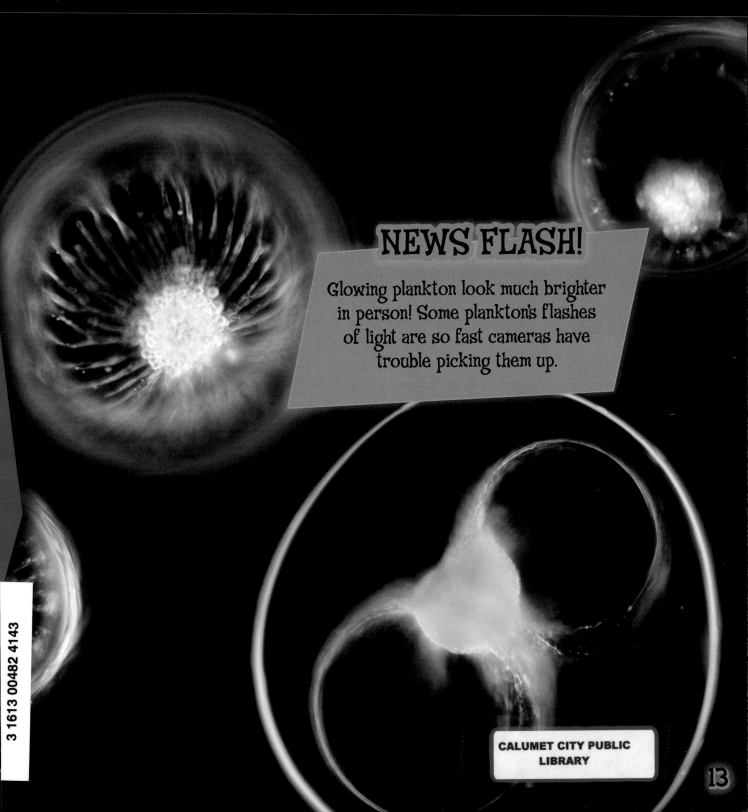

NEWS FLASH!

Glowing plankton look much brighter in person! Some plankton's flashes of light are so fast cameras have trouble picking them up.

13

SPARKLING AND SHOOTING GOO

Many glowing plankton are a type of algae called dinoflagellates. Because dinoflagellates are a kind of algae, they're considered a phytoplankton. Dinoflagellates are the most common form of bioluminescent plankton. One kind of dinoflagellate called a sea sparkle glows when it's moved by waves or other things in the water.

Some plankton can't make themselves glow, but they have another defense from predators. They shoot glowing goo into the water when predators are nearby. These gobs of goo confuse fish wanting to eat plankton.

Dinoflagellates, such as the sea sparkles shown here, are the most common bioluminescent creatures in the open ocean.

NEWS FLASH!

Dinoflagellates have two flagella, which are thin, movable body parts that help them swim. These help dinoflagellates spin as they move forward.

HUNGRY PLANKTON

What do plankton eat? It depends on the kind of plankton. Zooplankton commonly eat single-**celled** organisms or tiny plants.

Many phytoplankton make their own food. They do this through a process called photosynthesis, which takes energy from the sun and uses it to make food. These types of plankton include algae. Like plants, phytoplankton let out oxygen during photosynthesis. Animals need this gas to live.

Plankton are at the bottom of the food chain in ocean **habitats**. They're eaten by many different fish, which means they're important to many different animals, including people who eat fish!

Scientists don't think plankton use bioluminescence to help them find food. They use it to keep themselves from getting eaten by animals such as this crab.

MAKING PLANKTON AND SEA FOAM

Different kinds of plankton reproduce, or make more plankton, in different ways. Some reproduce on their own by putting **spores** into the water. Some split in half to make two plankton. Others need male and female plankton to come together and make babies. Most plankton can reproduce very quickly.

When plankton die, their bodies break down in the water. The dead plankton clump together to make sea foam. Sea foam forms when the wind and waves churn and whip the water around to create floating, soap-like bubbles. The sea foam sits on top of the water and is blown around by the wind.

NEWS FLASH!

A very quick increase in a plankton population is called a bloom.

Sea foam is so light that it can be blown onto land.

SEEING THE LIGHTS

People travel many miles to see glowing plankton on beaches at night. Bioluminescent Bay in Puerto Rico is famous for giving tours of its glowing shorelines. It's believed that up to 720,000 glowing plankton are in a single gallon of water from Bioluminescent Bay!

All around the world, people take pictures of glowing waters and watch the ocean light up as they go for a moonlight swim. Many people even take underwater dives in the dark to get a better view of bioluminescent plankton glowing in deeper waters.

Looking for glowing plankton has become a popular thing to do in many places around the world.

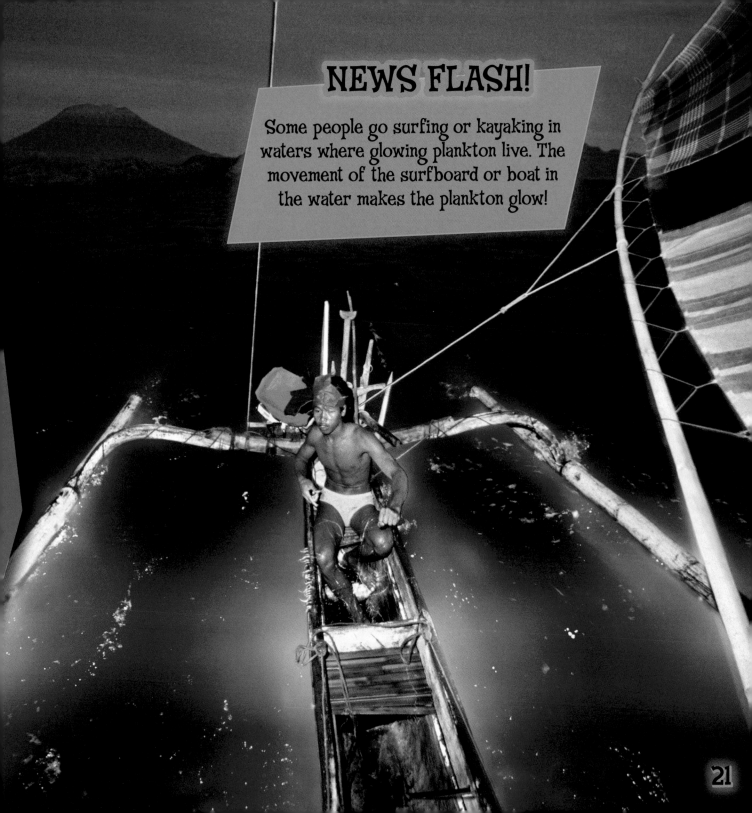

NEWS FLASH!

Some people go surfing or kayaking in waters where glowing plankton live. The movement of the surfboard or boat in the water makes the plankton glow!

21

FUN PLANKTON FACTS

1. Plankton are hunted by some predators that are also bioluminescent, such as lantern fish.

2. Some species of plankton go closer to the surface of the water at night and go deeper when the sun is out. This is called vertical migration.

3. Plankton glow blue and green because those colors of light are seen best in water.

4. In very deep parts of the ocean, bioluminescence is the only kind of light.

5. Phytoplankton populations decrease when the water's surface gets warmer.

GLOSSARY

algae: Small, plantlike organisms that grow in water.

attract: To bring close.

cell: The smallest basic part of a living thing.

chemical: Matter mixed with other matter to create change.

habitat: A place or type of place where a plant or animal usually lives.

microscope: An instrument that uses lenses to show detail in very small objects.

organism: A living thing.

process: A series of actions or changes.

shallow: Not deep.

spore: A small, seedlike body that can grow into a new organism.

INDEX

A

algae, 6, 10, 14

B

bioluminescence, 10, 12, 14, 16, 20, 22

Bioluminescent Bay, 20

bloom, 18

D

dinoflagellates, 14, 15

F

food, 16

food chain, 16

L

light flashes, 12, 13

M

macroplankton, 8, 9

microplankton, 9

N

nannoplankton, 8, 9

P

photosynthesis, 16

phytoplankton, 6, 9, 14, 16, 22

predators, 12, 14, 22

R

reproduction, 18

S

sea foam, 18, 19

sea sparkle, 14

species, 4, 22

Z

zooplankton, 6, 9, 16

WEBSITES